T0063104

TY

Through Grandma's Eyes

VJ Washington

Order this book online at www.trafford.com
or email orders@trafford.com

Most Trafford titles are also available at major online book retailers.

I, VJ Washington, the writer of this book, am not an expert on medications
that are mentioned in this book. I have only shared what I have experienced,
after my grandson took these medications and how he reacted to them.

Printed in the United States of America.

ISBN: 978-1-4907-1802-6 (sc)
ISBN: 978-1-4907-1803-3 (hc)
ISBN: 978-1-4907-1804-0 (e)

Library of Congress Control Number: 2013919457

Trafford rev. 10/26/2013

www.trafford.com

North America & international
toll-free: 1 888 232 4444 (USA & Canada)
fax: 812 355 4082

Ty, the true story of a young boy, who is viewed as nothing less than amazing, intelligent and loving, "through his grandma's eyes".

Based on a true story, written by
Author, VJ Washington

This book is dedicated to my mom, Tracy; Nevaeh, my baby sister; Arthur Washington, Sr., my granddad, and VJ Washington, my grandma and author of my story. I love you all for always being there for me and for putting up with my mood swings, even though, I didn't know what was happening most of the time. We can only pray that God will fix me sooner than later. Grandma says he will, she trusts God.

Much love, Ty.

Prelude

Nothing could have prepared my mom, or my grandparents for my behavior that changed like the wind from day to day. No, from moment to moment. No one knew what to think, what to do or how to deal with me.

My name is Tyrique Malachi. My last name is not important at this point, because everyone calls me "Ty", from my baby sister Nevaeh, (NeNe) to my granddad (whom I adore). Later, you will understand why.

I am telling this story in the hopes of helping parents who face the same situations that my family do, and I will give hope to them and their young children who like me, just don't understand what to do about their situations.

Don't be confused if I sometimes speak in the third person, because I will be telling my story, "through grandma's eyes".

Interlude

"Ty" Through Grandma's Eyes

This story is about a boy by the name of Ty, short for Tyrique. Ty was born on April 22, 2008 to his mom, Tracy and his dad, who we will mention at a later time. From the day of his birth, a "C" section, his mom felt he was strong, determined and blessed. He was born with his thumb in his mouth.

His grandma prayed for him to be happy, humble and healthy. Ty was a good baby, hardly ever cried. He sat up and also started crawling backwards at an early age. When Ty was 7 months old, his Granddad would hold Ty's legs and he would pull up into a sitting position without using his hands. He couldn't even walk yet, but he would perform this activity over and over again. He was strong. As he began to grow, Ty was always trying things out, never afraid of anything.

When he and his mom lived in Virginia, before the age of 1, his dad bought him a little tike, bike. Ty would stand on top of the seat with no hands, then put 1 leg back like he was about to fly and would not even fall. This frightened us. Where did he get that from? We looked and filmed and could not believe our eyes.

So many different phenomenal things stunned us about Ty, but we'll mention them as the story is told.

Chapter One

Prior to age one, Ty was sucking his thumb. Sometimes he would not eat his food because he just wanted to suck his thumb.

Mom had to try several different milks for him, because he was born with acid reflux and couldn't keep most milks down.

Ty's final milk was Continental 8, a soymilk. But we didn't know that, that was probably adding to his stomach pains that he often complained about.

Ty loved milk, but was always saying that his stomach was hurting.

By the age of eight months, Ty was walking, and going to the bathroom on his own, by age 1.

While living in Virginia with his mom and dad, Ty's dad trained him to go to the bathroom.

His dad would take his diaper off when Ty was at home and he knew not to wet on the floor.

So Ty had to say potty and his dad would go with him to the potty. He had bonded with his dad.

By the time Ty was about to have his first birthday party, Tracy, Ty's mom and Ty moved to Georgia to get help from her parents with Ty.

Ty's dad stayed behind, but he came to Georgia to Ty's birthday party. He bought a matching outfit for him and Ty.

Unfortunately, that would be the last time Ty had a party with his dad present.

There were many people who came to share in Ty's celebration at his first birthday party.

I counted 60 guests between family, children and friends. A happy time for Ty as he opened presents, though he didn't understand what the fuss was all about.

Shortly after the party, Ty's dad went back to Virginia and from then on, was not available.

After the party, Ty always looked for his dad, but no dad. What could be going through his mind as he would sit, stare and suck his thumb?

He would say "dada"? "no dada". Ty seemed so different and lonely. He was always a happy little boy prior to not seeing his dad. He would smile, laugh, and was playful. Tracy tried to fill the void. Taking up the slack of Mom and Dad.

Ty was placed in a nursery school where he would cry and didn't want Tracy to leave him.

Something happened at the first nursery and Tracy moved Ty to another nursery, a recommended Day Care Provider.

Now Ty is almost two, walking and talking a bit much and better. Ty was injured at this Day Care, so Tracy found another one for her little boy.

So many changes, but if she felt her son was in danger, she would move him to a safe haven until she found out otherwise.

Tracy played with her son and made him happy for a moment, but then the sad face, and finger sucking continued as he sat in a corner on her couch in her modest apartment. What could Ty be thinking?

Ty loved to help his mom. He would get his clothes out of the drawer. His mom would tell him where to look in his room and what to get. He knew exactly what she said and would do just just that.

He watched his mom as she cooked, cleaned and prepared his clothes.

It was just Ty and mom at home and he had his mom's attention. They would watch movies together, play puzzles, games, and Ty would take his finger out of his mouth long enough to put it together.

Ty could see a puzzle on a box, take it apart and put it back together with no help.

He always went to a daycare or nursery at someone's home care center.

Ty was learning. He caught on fast. He mumbled words early on and we thought he would have a speech impediment.

Ty cried a lot when his mom left him each morning, but Tracy knew she was the bread winner of the family and had to make her money to take care of her and her son. So she tried not to let him see her concern of leaving him.

Soon after Ty turned one, Tracy realized that she was pregnant from Ty's dad with his sister Nevaeh.

As she grew in her pregnancy, Ty would touch Tracy's stomach and say sista, baby? As Tracy would let him know he was going to have a baby sister.

When the new baby, Nevaeh was born, Ty went through some changes as boys do with their younger sisters.

He always wanted to hold her, to kiss her and sit beside her on the floor or couch.

He used to pull on her arm as though she could walk and wanted mommy to sit her in his lap.

Tracy worked with Ty as much as she could. But it wouldn't be long before he showed a different side. He was acting out, crying, wetting on himself, talking back, being stubborn.

Tracy always informed the doctor of his behavior. She was told that he was just stubborn and would grow out of it.

At school, he would cry, try to follow Tracy out the door and wet on himself during the day. He would always come home with a dirty bag and a different set of clothes.

Chapter Two

February 1, 2010, Nevaeh Destiny was born by a "C" section, Tracy's second birth by "C" Section.

Another beautiful and phenomenal child, but that's another story. She had a strawberry patch on her forehead, just like her paternal grandmother in Virginia.

Grandma prayed for Nevaeh too, to be happy, humble and healthy. I love my grandmother, she is a remarkable lady.

And she tells me how wonderful I am all the time.

Now I am two and "through grandma's eyes", I am amazing. As my sister got older, my mom put both of us in a nursery, where they had room for the two of us.

She always wanted us to stay together. Shortly after our move to this nursery, something went wrong and mommy placed me and Nevaeh at another day care.

Nevaeh never cried when mom left us. I was missing my mom and I cried for her all the time. So I would suck my thumb and play by myself as a safe measure, until mommy came for me and Vaeh.

The Director of the nursery placed us in different rooms according to our age group.

When I would see NeNe, as I called my sister, I would run to her and give her a great big hug and kiss, and she would return the same to me. I love my sister. You would think we were twins.

It's just me, mom and NeNe. But I am sad sometimes. Grandma would notice my sad face and ask "what's wrong Ty"? But granddad would say, a'int nothing wrong with that boy, stop making a sissy out of him.

Now, I didn't know what a sissy was, but I would soon say "you sissy"!

Grandma said, "that's not nice Ty, don't say that". But I would reply, "but granddaddy says it".

Grandma says, "some things you don't need to repeat. You are bright, sweet and a good boy". I noticed she would always change the subject when things seemed out of control.

I didn't know what he meant, but granddad called me a mama's boy because I always went to grandma when I felt uncomfortable.

She would make me feel like a big boy by comforting and encouraging me, and I would stop crying and feel better as she hugged me.

Two years old and I am feeling lost, "through grandma's eyes". "Something is wrong with Ty", she would say to my mom, and mom would just say, "the doctor says he's just stubborn".

I wouldn't budge sometimes when my granddad called me. He would have to count to 3 and I would move before he got his belt. I knew I didn't want to get the belt on my behind.

Mom saw that I was stubborn and talking back, besides that, I would not listen when I was spoken to. I would move slow and just not do what I was told.

Grandma also noticed the change in me and said "Something is wrong with Ty, he needs to see a Psychiatrist".

Tracy, was always on the ball. She had already been going to sessions for her and Ty, and of course they only heard what he had been doing but never saw him act out.

He would just suck his thumb like a good boy and seem very well behaved. Isn't that something.

Chapter Three

By now, the doctor had prescribed some medicine for Ty as he had been acting out.

Grandma says, "It has to be the medicine. He is changing and getting worse. He wets his pants at night. He won't go to the bathroom during the day.

It's always", "I don't' have to" or "I can't". Even to take a bath, it's, "I can't".

I recall even as young as two years old, when grandma felt I understood what she was saying, she would take me upstairs to her prayer room.

Grandma would lay her hands on my forehead and say. "Let's pray", then she would explain what we prayed about.

Grandma believed that you should follow Proverbs 22:6 Train up a child in the way he should go and when he is old, he would not part from it.

She always said "look at me", she said, "when you talk to people, look them in the eyes, so you can understand what they are trying to say to you".

I always felt better when we came down from the prayer room. I felt like a big boy, doing was I was told to do.

Grandma did not want to see me get in trouble, but sometimes my tummy would hurt me, I couldn't use the bath room and granddaddy thought I just wouldn't try.

Later I would need to go to the bathroom and change my clothes. Granddaddy would be so angry at me.

Granddaddy said, "that's what's wrong with these boys today, mothers and grandmothers are always making a sissy out of them". I don't like for granddaddy to call me a sissy.

When mommy takes me and Vaeh to the stores, I act out. Sometimes I knock things off the shelf and scream "no" when she tells me to stop.

Sometimes I am so bad that she has to call granddad to come from wherever he is and get me. Remind you, she has Vaeh to carry and see after. She tries to deal with both of us but I don't know why I don't listen, but when grandad shows up, I cry, suck my thumb and move slowly towards the car where granddad instructed me to go.

Mom gave me medicine before we went to the store, but the medicine seemed to have made me behave worse. I don't understand why I am so mad and angry.

I have nose bleeds, so when I act out and overheat, I have a nose bleed. Mom is so embarrassed, she wants to give up, but grandma keeps telling her that "God made you strong", and "it will be alright after while".

Grandma says, "you won't know what it could have been like if you give up". I love for my grandma to pray for us.

I know God hears her prayers, at least that's what she tells me. I believe grandma.

Chapter Four

Mom takes us to our grandparents every weekend because she has to work a double. She has to make money to pay the rent.

She tells me that she does not like to be away so much but she has to take care of us. I love mommy, though she thinks I don't because of the way I behave.

Mommy says, "come on Ty, let's take your bath", I reply, "I can't, can you take me a bath", mommy says "no, you are four, you can take your own bath". I cry, "I can't, I don't know how".

After a little while, mommy comes in, shows me how to use the soap and towel again, and tells me to rinse off and get out.

She gets so frustrated with me and tells me to go to my room because I am crying, that she won't help me put my clothes on. I sit on the bed and cry and suck my thumb. I soon fall asleep.

NeNe has taken her bath, gotten dressed and is ready for bed by herself, at two years old. She is smart.

I'm glad that tomorrow we will be going to my grandparent's home so we can play outside.

I love my granddad. When he is feeling like it, he takes me outside and shows me how to water the plants that he planted. I like the outdoors. I feel free.

Granddad allows Vaeh to come too. He can't go too many places without her. She always says, "where's my granddad?, I was supposed to go with him".

When he moves to go out the door, she will run and grab her doll baby and her shoes and almost beat him out the door, shouting, "don't leave me".

He planted some pecan trees and peaches in his yard and he let me water each one. I think its about 8 or 10 of them.

He says, I did a great job and he has to pay me.

When granddad gives me money, he takes me to "Toys R Us" or the dollar store and let's me pick out a toy, usually a toy car. He would also bring NeNe, and buy her a little doll or something she could play with.

Granddad lets me and NeNe pluck his whiskers and gives us a dollar. He also lets us brush his hair. He is so much fun to be around.

When he sits in his big yellow chair, NeNe and I argue over who will sit in Granddad's lap. So Granddad sits on the floor and allows the two of us to sit on either side of him.

He plays pick up sticks with us and we always sit by granddad and watch the TV movie "24" or Criminal Minds and Burn Notice.

Granddad explains what the story is about and tells us what we should do or not do.

Usually grandma is on the internet or cooking or cleaning until time for us to get ready for bed. But she plays with us sometimes. She does the match games, tic tac toe and teaches us our numbers on the flash cards.

Grandma buys us puzzles every now and then so we can separate them and put them back together. She said that is great concentration for the mind.

Mommy drops us off early on Saturday morning to our grandparent's house. When grandma opens the door and says good morning, we say good morning and dart straight to the bedroom where granddaddy is still sleeping.

Then the day begins. I try to dominate the TV by watching "SpongeBob". Grandma doesn't seem to care. It keeps us still for a while. Then we ask to eat breakfast, and to go outside.

Mommy always gives us pancakes and sausage or bagels and we come here and want to eat cereal. I can't have milk because it tends to constipate me, so when I ask for cereal here, grandma let's me have milk, but not too much.

My baby sister, Nevaeh says, "are you serious, Ty is not suppose to have milk. Mommy said no milk for Ty". "I'm telling on all of y'all". But grandma allows a little for both of us. I am grateful.

She just wants me to be happy and hopes that the little bit does not affect me.

Plus she says if "he's hungry, let him eat", because my appetite is not good due to the medicine that I take.

Mommy says she is working on another appointment for me with a Psychiatrist. But the Psychiatrist has to talk to my medical doctor to see why I have become so aggressive. She does not want to change my medicine again.

Mommy saw how I have been different without anything, so prayerfully, I won't need anything especially when I start my new school in August. Everyone is hoping that I stay busy and focused.

I love to stay busy, the problem is staying focused. I had to take an entrance test for public school to see if I was ready to go to kindergarten.

The principal says I scored high. I am a smart boy like grandma always says. Time will show everyone and I know grandma's prayers are being answered.

Chapter Five

I am five. Mommy had a party for me. We invited some of my friends from school and my Goddy Darlene and Goddy Benji came to the party too.

I had a great time at my party. Some of mommy's friends came and brought me toys, of course, they brought NeNe something too. I didn't mind.

I'm a big boy, my grandma vacuums her floors. I always want to help, so I ask grandma to let me do it.

She is happy to have me help her, because she can move on to something else, like washing clothes, dishes and ironing the clothes.

Grandma works hard. She goes to work on her regular job, then she comes home, cooks, cleans and sometimes takes care of us through the week, with the help of granddad.

I love staying at my grandparent's home because they have Wi-Fi and I can download games on grandma's phone.

My granddad bought me and Vaeh a touch pad. We were able to decide which one we wanted. I asked her to take the bigger one because she could hold it better. I took the much smaller one.

She is always agreeable to what I ask her to do. When I don't want to get into trouble, I will tell NeNe to do something and she loves to make me happy.

Sometimes I get caught telling her and I do get into trouble.

My granddad is always finding things to keep our minds focused. We told granddad thank you and grandma too.

Sometimes I am not happy because I want to play the games all day, and my grandparents said we have to take a break from the devices, such as cell phones and I-pads.

I begin to act out when they take them. They just don't understand. It keeps me calm. But they want me to do other activities, like my homework.

Grandma says, "lets go outside before you get in trouble Ty". But I want to play the games on her phone.

I say, "no, I'm not going outside, I want to play the games". Granddad steps in and begins to count to 3 or tells me to go in the room.

I'm crying so hard while sucking my thumb. "Take that finger out of your mouth and go in the room", he says.

NeNe aggravates the situation.

"Granddaddy, Ty won't go in the room".

"No, I can't". Boy, look out. Granddad is military and is not having it, my stubborn behavior.

He makes me go in the room, where I kick the door, scream and holler.

He comes in the room and whacks me on the behind. I wet on myself.

Granddad says, "go clean yourself up and change your clothes".

"No, I can't". Another whack with the belt. Then I go clean up and granddad has fixed a pallet for me to take a nap.

Lights out, me, my tears and my finger.

When I wake up, grandma gives me something to eat. I like peanut butter sandwiches, so peanut butter it is, and they give me my medicine for the afternoon.

I don't think the medicine is working, but grandma takes me and Vaeh outside, because now I am getting into trouble. We ride our bikes, and other toys.

Sometimes grandma throws the ball to us, or Vaeh and I play together.

Today, while we were outside riding our bikes, we call our Goddy, Mr. Benji down to play with us. He just lives down the street and he was sitting on his porch.

Whenever we call him or Mrs. Darlene, they will come. Sometimes he helps me make airplanes, he also helps me fly my kite.

Mr. Benji once took a wheel off my bike so I could learn to ride it, but got scared when I almost fell off, and said, "not on my watch, will Ty get hurt". So he put the wheel back on.

Grandma, as protective as she is of me and NeNe, decided to take the wheels off and let me go for it. She held me for a while, then said, "keep your head up and put your foot down if you feel yourself falling".

I got the concept in one day, and now I am riding my bike without wheels. Thank you grandma. I love you.

For two weeks, I was due to go to the new school for two hours a day, so that the teachers could see how I would take the challenge, of changing schools and see if I was ready to write my name.

Well, the medicine seem to have made me aggressive and act out. The doctor had just switched me to (Cyproheptadine). This medication is to treat unusual behavior and diarrhea.

When mom dropped me off on her way to work, I started kicking, fighting the teachers and knocking down anything in my way.

It took 3 or 4 school personnel to get me to calm down. I am not a bad boy. I just don't understand what is happening to me.

At night when we visit my grandparents, they always ask what kind of day we had.

This particular day, the doctors had changed my medicine to (Concerta). This medicine is to treat ADHD. It may cause abdominal pain, dry mouth (thirstiness), headaches and irritability, all of which I experienced.

And I am getting ready to go to big school. I don't take change well.

I had another episode at school. Not listening and fighting with the teachers.

They had to calm me down again.

Granddad had to go out of town on business, grandma had to go to work and mommy had to take me home with her for the night.

That evening, after mom picked us up from school she brought me and Vaeh to visit with grandma because she was alone while granddad was out of town.

We ate fish sticks and potatoes, one of my favorite meals.

When it was almost time for us to go home, I told mommy to come with me to the bathroom, she told me to go by myself, that I was a big boy.

I said, "no, I booboo on myself, I told you to come with me". Mommy was calm. She cleaned me up and said "let's go so you can take a bath at home".

I didn't want to eat because I was playing games on grandma's phone. So when mommy got ready to go, I was hungry. She said, "too bad, let's go, you can eat when we get home".

I said "no, I want to eat now".

Mommy was fed up with me talking back.

She started leaving out the door with our stuff to go home. I was not budging. I said, "I am not going home, I'm staying here with grandma".

Mrs. Darlene had come over to visit us. She tried to talk to me but I said "no". My bossy, 3 year old sister was screaming in my ear, "boy, let's go, now". I said "no, leave me alone".

By the third time she screamed at me and said, "let's go now, mommy said let's go", I pushed her down.

Grandma called her away and told her to let Mrs. Darlene deal with me. Then everyone went outside, but I didn't want to go home.

There is no Wi-Fi and I was at my grandparent's home. I had been there for two weeks because I would not listen to mommy and was talking back.

When I wouldn't go outside, grandma stepped outside. I followed her, then she suddenly turned and quickly closed the door as she went back inside.

I started fighting anyone who tried to make me get in mommy's car. I ran back to the house, grandma tried to stay away from me, knowing I would try to stay. I hit the door so hard, she thought I broke my hand.

I would not get in the car and kept yelling, fighting, kicking, and wearing my mom and Mrs. Darlene out. Grandma turned the lights out at her house. Mommy was at her wits end. She could not handle me, so she called the cops.

The last time she tried to make me get in the car, I started kicking at the window, fighting my sister in the back seat and mom had to turn around and come back to granddad. That's when she left me there for a week.

I want to be a police officer when I grow up. So the police came and tried to get me out of the car where I had finally settled.

I was crying so hard and would not budge. The police officer tried talking to me for 45 minutes. I was not going to get out of the car. I told them that I would "bust the windows out, pee on myself and other stuff. I was angry that I could not stay at grandma's home.

I am so mad now. No one understands me. I want my granddad, and he is out of town.

Finally, I tired myself out, long enough for mommy to drive home, but I was still crying.

When we got home, I would not get out of the car. Mommy had to deal with my baby sister too. I didn't care, I wanted my grandparents. Mommy called the cops. After awhile, I decided to go up the stairs at the apartments where we lived, still crying and mad. But at least a little calmer.

Mommy had me get in the tub.

After I bathed, she sent me to my room to think about my behavior. I don't know what happened. Still angry and confused, I went to sleep, sucking my thumb.

At school the next day, I listened, participated and had a beautiful day.

Mommy told me how proud she was and took me and Vaeh to Chick-Fila, one of my favorite places to eat.

It's the weekend again. My Goddy is so concerned about me. She is always telling mommy and grandma about the medications that I am taking. She says don't put me on no medication, try to

19

deal with him. Mommy reads up on them but says I have to have them, though she hopes I grow out of my illness as my primary doctor said, "he's just stubborn".

Yesterday, grandma let us play in the water slide in her front yard. NeNe and I had so much fun. We tired ourselves out, but when it was time to go inside, I said "no", so grandma left me outside while she took NeNe inside and gave her a bath, she kept checking on me though. I was looking around, and sucking my thumb, because I was outside all alone.

I finally went inside, took a bath and simmered down. After that Grandma took us to our Goddy house down the street.

Goddy called and said that while she and Mr. Benji was down the street cutting someone's yard, someone broke into her storage in her back yard and stole a piece of equipment, in broad daylight.

Goddy called the police, but they did not even take fingerprints. And she wondered if it was just a waste of her time to have called them. Goddy thinks she knows who did it.

When we were playing down at Goddy, I knocked my sister's earring out of her ear by mistake. Everyone started looking in the grass for it.

Grandma said, "come look for it Ty, you have a good eye". I told her, "I'm not going to look for it, I'm the one who knocked it out of her ear".

My persistent grandma kept looking until she found it in the grass. Then Goddy went to look for who she thought stole her equipment.

They had me and NeNe get in the back seat of the car. I cried. I didn't want to go the other way, I wanted to go back to grandma's house. So I started saying "no, I don't want to go". Then I kept hitting my sister in the back seat. She was crying, but I didn't care. Grandma hollered at me to stop. I said, "no, take me home".

When we got back home, it was nighttime. We were cleaned up for bed. I fell asleep. Granddad said, "Ty you had a lot of water, get up and go to the bathroom", I said, "no, I can't, I don't have to".

We went through this for a while back and forward. Granddaddy said, "you wet my blanket, no outside for you tomorrow and I'm going to spank your behind".

I kept laying there, cuddled up, and sucking my thumb. I've done this several times before. Through the night, I did wet the blanket, but I got up before granddad. I cleaned myself up and grandma washed the blanket after she fussed at me.

My grandma doesn't like a lot of discord. So she just tries to keep the peace. They tell me how my 3 year old sister sleeps in her underwear, and doesn't wet the bed while I wear pull-ups at night and wets the bed.

Mommy said, "don't give him anything to drink before he goes to bed, it's a part of his condition, he will wet on himself".

I don't know, I'm confused. I don't like to get up and go to the bathroom through the night, that's what grandma says.

Sometimes I wet myself at school or at grandma's house. Mom knows because I have on a complete change of clothes. Is it me being lazy, or is it the medicine?

I had a rough day again on yesterday.

Mommy planned a good outing for Vaeh, me and my grandparents. We were all going to take a family portrait. Mommy planned this family portrait a long time ago.

Something happened. Granddaddy got tired of standing, waiting, so he decided to walk through Walmart. I had to follow him.

Now it's our turn to take pictures.

We could not be found. So mommy and Vaeh took a picture together. Then grandma said, "let's just do a girl's 3 generation. So mommy, Vaeh and grandma took pictures.

Mommy and grandma were so upset that we missed our appointment. But we can make another appointment another time.

I started acting out in granddaddy's truck on the way home. We had just come back from McDonald's. I was throwing french fries at NeNe and hitting her.

Mommy screamed for me to leave her alone. I screamed back, then she hit me.

I don't always listen to mommy, that's why I have to go to bed early sometimes. Mommy sends me to my room to think about what I did wrong.

As grandma always says. "It will be alright".

Well, it's Monday, and my first day at the big school for kindergarteners. I had a great day. Only one thing, I forgot to take my lunch money out of my book bag during lunch. Mommy had told me what to do that morning.

I forgot and the teachers can't touch my things, so nobody gave me any food to eat at lunch time.

Well, they want me to be more responsible so, a few more days of this and I will remember to get my money out. (sad face).

Chapter Six

Grandma says, "something has to be done, we can't just keep imagining if Ty is going to outgrow this behavior. He is getting worse as he gets older.

Sometimes she wants me to be on the medicine so mommy and I can have a great day, but she considers that in the long run it is not good for me physically or mentally. Because it could do damage to my body and mind.

Now my doctor has prescribed (Adderall/Intuniv). The side affects are stomach pain, low blood pressure, tiredness and trouble sleeping.

I never had a problem falling asleep before. When I take my bath and settle down on the couch, I suck my thumb and fall fast asleep.

Prior to this medication, I was taking Methylphenidate a form of Ritalin (Concerta). This medicine causes aggression, stomach pain, loss of appetite and affects chemicals in the brain. It treats ADHD, and bipolar patients. It causes insomnia and the individual experiences extreme mood swings.

Mom says she is trying. But she doesn't know what else to do. Grandma says, "it will be alright". We will keep working with him, while trying to find help.

My mom just wants to have a little peace in her home and for us to have peace too. Grandma prays a lot for all of us.

Grandma says she has spoken to social workers who visits students at her school, and other grandparents whose grands have behavior problems like mine.

They don't know what to do either.

The psychologist says he will grow out of it, but you may have to put him on medication.

I explained that Ty was on medication. That it was not working, only seemed to give him aches and pains and it makes him very aggressive.

Ty is not a bad child, in fact when he is having a good day, he will try to explain to his sister how things should be and sometimes he will switch to a totally different person all of a sudden and want to hit her and make her cry.

He would push her away, snatch things from her, hit her and then fuss you out when you tell him about his behavior.

I am convinced that he has a chemical imbalance, but what can we do about it. The different medicines all have terrible side affects.

Grandma takes me upstairs to her prayer room when she knows I will pay attention to her. She lays her hand on my head and ask God to heal me. And to give mommy peace.

When we come down from the prayer room, I feel calm, and then I ask grandma if I could play with her phone. (manipulative).

Granddad gave Vaeh and me some paper so we could write our name. I can spell Tyrique, but I have a problem writing "y" and "q". Granddaddy said, "look at the letters, you are writing them backwards". So I keep trying and I finally got it.

Granddaddy took my sister and me to my uncle Art's house. He has lots of animals; fish, horses, dogs, chickens. We love to visit his home.

But today, uncle Art invited us to come over and see his new "go cart". He has a lot of land. He rode us on it. We had fun. Then Granddaddy took us to another one of our favorite places to eat, "McDonalds". Granddaddy thinks he doesn't spoil us, but he does.

Today, mommy came home early from work. We are not ready to go home.

She took me and Vaeh outside to play ball with us while at my grandparent's home.

Mommy is not an outside person.

That was so cool and different for her and us. And we all had fun. Thank you mommy.

After we played, ate grandma's cooking, now it was time to go home.

Mommy says "put your shoes on, clean up your mess and let's go". I reply, "no, I am not going anywhere, I'm still staying right here". I don't want to leave my grandparents home.

NeNe says, "boy, let's go right now, mommy is ready to go". I just didn't pay her any attention, I said, "no, I'm still eating my food".

Granddaddy said, "come on buddy, I'll walk you to the car". Well, I got up to go home, this time without a fight.

If I could, I would never go home, I just want to stay here. Grandma says, maybe when school starts, things would be different. With all the interaction with the bigger kids and the new activities at school.

I love mommy, like I told grandma up in the prayer room, but I want to play my IPod that granddaddy bought and mommy does not have Wi-Fi.

Grandma used to let me download games on her phone, then all of a sudden she stopped. She said it takes up too much space on her phone. Man, now I have to find something else to do.

Today, it was so hot, but grandma let us ride our bikes outside then she said we were sweating, come inside. I asked if we could play in the garage with the door down. She said yes, for a little while. So we rode our bikes and played ball.

Suddenly, the light fell down from the ceiling. That scared me and NeNe. We ran inside to grandma. NeNe told grandma that I threw the ball up and hit the light. Grandma was mad at me. I cried and said, "I didn't do that, she is not telling the truth". "Yes he did", NeNe said. Grandma cleaned the mess up and made us go inside. I was angry.

Last night Mommy had to go to the grocery store. Grandma had to get her car from my mom. So granddad picked us up from the store and went to mommy's house for a little while.

Mommy fed me and Vaeh mac and cheese and steak tips. I didn't want that. I told mommy I was not going to eat that and I wanted a popsicle too.

Mommy was not hearing it. She gave Vaeh a bath, told me to take mine. I said "no, I'm not taking a bath here, I'm going to granddad's house".

Mommy said "you are not and stop talking back to me". I was playing upside down on the couch. I fell and hit my head.

I ran to grandma crying. Mommy was right. She just said, "sit up right on the couch before you fall and hit your head".

When granddad got ready to go, mommy said "say good night and give, grandma and granddad a kiss". I started walking towards the door, sucking my thumb.

Granddad said, "go back inside".

"No, I said, I'm going to your house, I am not staying here". Granddad kept walking out mommy's door. I followed him down to the parking lot with no shoes on.

Mommy was so upset with me.

"Take him, she said", but granddad convinced me to go upstairs and take a bath. By this time mommy gave me some calming medicine and I was able to simmer down, relax, then I fell asleep.

"TY"

I am Ty, a little boy who grandma says is very bright.

I love to laugh, I love to play and kiss my mom and sister good night.

My babysister is adorable too, she makes me happy when she is around.

But sometimes she bothers things that are mine, and I hit her and hit her or push her to the ground.

Though granddad is not my dad, I know, He shows great strength and love for me and mommy, she tries so hard, but she just can't deal with me.

Grandma, she prays and prays and prays and tells everyone, that things will change so God, please do what you do best and let us see the change come soon.

Chapter Seven

Today, I'm praying for a great day for Ty. Tracy said for the past two days that he was with her, she didn't give him any of his medicine and he actually had great days at school. Even the teacher and the Head Master said "is that Tyrique"?

Again, the Head Master told my granddad that he is shocked at my behavior. Little does he know how I behaved last night.

We went to the store again this evening. Mommy had to pick up a few things. She has to go when she has a ride because her car is still being worked on. I am going to grandma's house.

When we arrived, grandma gave me and Vaeh a peanut butter and jelly sandwich. I love the peanut butter. Vaeh loves both.

When we were waiting for mom to come out of the store, NeNe said "I guess I am beating you Ty with my apple pie". I told her, "you can't beat me, I don't have an apple pie, I have a peanut butter sandwich".

Grandma let me fix another sandwich until the food was done. I told grandma, that I only wanted chicken and rice.

Grandma said, it's not chicken Ty, I said, "I mean ox tails then".

Granddaddy asked me to fix him a peanut butter sandwich. I did, and grandma went to her spot in the other room to get on the computer until the food was ready.

I'll be staying here for a little while again. Grandma will be ironing my outfits for the rest of the week. She loves for my clothes to be pressed, like mommy does.

They say I look like a little man.

I hope mommy get her car soon. She likes taking us to Zaxbys and Chick-Fila.

My mommy is such a nice mom. Also, when we are happy, mommy is happy too.

It's morning at grandma and granddad. Time to get up, Ty wants to look at SpongeBob. NeNe wants to look at her movie that her mommy rented for her, "Incredible Ivan".

After an episode of SpongeBob, I told Ty to change it up and let NeNe watch her program. Then the fighting began. He does not like change and wants what he wants.

"Okay", I said, nobody looks at TV and turned it off. "No, stop", says Ty, "I want to look at my program". Well, I'm not having it, so let's get your medicine".

I tried not to have to give it to him today.

I gave him the 5 mg of Adderall.

And prayed that God works this behavior problem out soon.

Romans 8:28 And we know that [a] God causes all things to work together for good to those who love God, to those who are called according to His purpose

I believe while we continue to seek help, when Ty starts school, he will be a different child, because he will have a more structured setting and will want to participate in what the other kids are doing.

While we are told that the diagnosis of "bipolar" runs in the family, I have two brothers who have mental illnesses as well.

One brother who is 61 years old and has been in a facility for the mentally challenged since the age of 9, is a ward of the state of Florida.

The other brother is 76, he is self sufficient, and lives with a relative in Florida. Only their illnesses are not hereditary.

Though we are not putting labels on my grandson, we do recognize that he has some challenges that he and we have to learn to overcome. And with God on our side, this too shall pass.

These are some of the different medicines that Ty has been on since the age of three. Dextraphetamine 5 mg 4/2011; Cyproheptadine 4 mg 7/12, Intunive for Bipolar 6/13; Concerta 6/13; Methylphenidate 18 mg 7/13; Adderall 7/13 Adderall (higher dosage) 9/13.

When it appears that the medicine does not work for Ty anymore or his behavior changes drastically, Tracy would notify the doctor to see why, and what could be done to correct his behavior.

She had an appointment in September with the Behavioral Therapist. We need help and we need it now. We will continue to persevere and pray for Ty and us.

Chapter Eight

August 5, 2013—school started
This was my first time riding on a school bus. Everyone told me to be a big boy. I had my book bag, my supplies and my new uniforms for the big school.

I am so blessed to have my Mom, my grandparents, and my maternal aunties, uncles and my cousin, Desiree.

They love me unconditionally. And when I need someone to share their opinions or come to my aid they are always there.

I love my family. They will never give up on me. I hope God blesses me soon, "through grandma's eyes".

Today, while at granddad's house, grandma said, "wow, what a kodak moment, grandson and granddad looking at movies together, sharing thoughts and ideas". I was sitting in granddad's lap.

If only this was everyday, all day. I asked grandma, if I could play her cell phone. She said, "no violent games".

"What does that mean?", I asked. She said, "no fighting with fists, guns and so on". "Oh", I replied.

I showed grandma that I was playing the hockey game and I only wanted to play one game. So she let me play for a while.

It's our anniversary today, August 1, 2013. Ty has pink eye and had to be out of school. He went with us to "I Hop" to breakfast. "Yeah, I love pancakes", he said.

"What's the name of that place again grandma", Ty asked.

I told him IHop. He asked for pancakes, but drank his orange juice and didn't eat his food. Then we headed out to the spa, a place my son recommended, called "Treat Your Feet", in Doraville, so granddad could get a treatment.

Besides being fidgety, Ty was actually pretty good for 1 full hour. But when it was time to go, he began acting out, wanting granddad to put his shoes on.

Granddad left him on the big couch in the spa, and came to the truck where I had already gone before them.

Ty came out with his shoes in his hands crying that he couldn't put his shoes on.

After a while, he fell off to sleep in the back of the truck, where we had to stop at another store.

When he awoke, he started crying that he didn't want to go to the store, he wanted to go home.

He cried in the store for a minute.

Then helped us find the corndogs that his Goddy always buys him from BJ's.

Another episode in the world of Ty.

But once he got home, he was in his safe space.

It's back to school this morning. Ty didn't want to get up. Said he didn't want to go to school.

I pulled him out of the bed and took him to the bathroom where he got cleaned up, and put on his clothes, while I reassured him that he was a big boy.

Granddad took him to school and we pray that he will have a great day.

My days have been good at school.

First I go to the Academy then the van takes me to the Elementary.

The teachers are learning me and I am learning the teachers. But the Elementary is so different from the Academy. We do a lot of stuff and it just tires me out, we don't take naps.

My granddad loves to take me to school. He picks me and Vaeh up from our home and drops us off at the Academy very early in the mornings. We love riding in granddad's big, white truck.

But a couple of days later, we went to my grandparents. I didn't want to go home. Mommy said I have to go home because I have to get up early and go to school.

I cried and stayed behind when it was time to go because I love staying at my grandparents' home.

Well, granddad walked me out to mommy's car and I went home. But I was not happy about that either.

My Goddy Darlene came to see how our first week was going. I told her that I like my new school. She was happy for me.

Grandma prayed that we both continue to have great days, NeNe and me.

Good days at school, short lived. Day 4 at my new school. The teacher sent a note home that I was talking a lot and not focusing. I am confused.

Mommy was very upset with me and fussed me out. She said I better keep my mouth shut and listen to the teacher.

They want me to take my finger out of my mouth and talk, but when I do talk, I'm talking too much.

Don't they realize that I am in a new surrounding, trying to find my way and trying to make new friends.

I am not a baby, I just want to make friends. Do I sit like a dummy with my finger in my mouth all day, or do I open up and try to be friendly?

I know I have to wait until I am allowed to talk, but just a day ago, I had all good reports of what a good boy I was at my new school. I don't understand.

Grandma told mommy that 1 day out of 179 or so days for the year is not bad if I learn from this, so don't worry too much, she said reassuring mom.

She said, she would talk to me this weekend, but try not to be too hard because at least I am talking.

Somebody please tell me, what am I suppose to do? I know that Ty is suffering from the absence of his father. This is why he loves hanging around his granddaddy. He mimmicks everything his granddady does, that he can do in front of him. And bottom line, Ty curls up in his granddad's lap and arms and receives the love that his granddaddy showers him with.

Dads must step up and be men to these boys. I remember the bond that Ty and his dad had for the first year of his life.

Unfortunately, the only dad NeNe knows is her granddad. But God will keep these two covered because I prayed and His loving hands are on these two little angels. I trust God.

Proverbs 3:5-6

5 Trust in the Lord with all your heart and lean not on your own understanding;
6 in all your ways submit to him, and he will make your paths straight.[a]

Chapter Nine

Granddaddy said he was going to take us to the beach, to Mississippi, Alabama, to visit Rosa Parks museum, and see other historic sites.

He always took my older cousin, Desiree to visit historic sites all over, from Rhode Island to Gatlinburg, Tennessee, when she was growing up.

She has all the states magnets on the West Coast, still on my grandparent's refrigerator, places where they stopped in each state, on the way to Rhode Island when she Desiree was very young.

My granddad loves to share things with me and Vaeh from hunting to fishing to different criminal shows and whatever he could explain to us, he does.

Grandma says every boy needs a male role model. Granddaddy is a great role model. When I grow up, I want to be like my granddaddy. I hug him and tell him, "I love you granddaddy", he says, "I love you too buddy", as he rubs my head, with my thumb in my mouth.

Mommy must be relaxing with me staying at my grandparents. I want her to have some peace and to bond with my baby sister. She is a hand full too you know.

So with only one at a time, mommy does not have to holler so much and she can get some rest as well. I love my mommy and my baby sister.

The more I assess my grandson, I am trying to see what triggers his condition and what keeps him calm.

Obviously, I can't get in his head, but I can try to figure out what I see with the naked eye, and let God do the rest.

I recall the day Ty and I were at his Goddy's house. We were at her table talking about "big school". Ty said, "I don't want to go to big school, it tires me out".

I could see that he was getting upset, so I took my phone, sat it on the table and was taping him. When he saw that I was bothering the phone and pushing it closer to him, (trying to get a clear view), Ty looked at me, then looked at the phone as if to say, "what are you doing with that?".

He gave me one funny look, or was he wondering, "I wonder if she will let me play with her phone". Because it did look as though I was pushing it towards him.

God is going to give us an answer soon, I have no doubt.

John 14:13-14

Whatever you ask in My name, that will I do, so that the Father may be glorified in the Son. 14"If you ask Me anything in My name, I will do it.

When I was at granddad's, He turned on the animal channel. We saw the dragons eat the deer, and try to kill the buffalo. They killed the deer with their poisonous venom and then ate them for dinner.

I had been sleep since we got to granddad's house. So when I woke up, grandma said, "it's time to take a bath". I didn't budge. Granddad said "go to the bathroom". I said "I already pee'd on myself, but I didn't pee in your chair because I was sitting on my leg". Granddad was not smiling. He said, "boy go take a bath".

Grandma wanted me to take a bath and put a pamper on, but I didn't want to because I am not a baby. She said, "well, babies wet their pants not 5 year olds".

And I asked grandma to stay in the bathroom while I took a bath because I was scared.

Grandma is going to retire soon and she will have more time to spend with us.

I am happy for her and for us.

Chapter Ten

Grandma took us outside for a little bit today, but it was too hot and she brought us back inside. I cried because I wanted to stay outside and play.

When grandma tried to put the garage down, I screamed because my truck was keeping it from closing, but I didn't want to move it, because I wanted to play outside.

Why do we have to go inside? NeNe and I love being outside, even in the hot sun. Mommy bought us something to spray on our body. But grandma said, "you can come back out later, after the sun goes down".

When mommy came from work, I told grandma I did not want to go home with mommy. She bought a red box movie to watch with us and then she took us to get ice cream.

Mommy is always buying things for us, trying to keep us happy as she spends quality time with us.

When we got back, we watched the movie for a while, then it got late and mom said she needed to go home and prepare for work tomorrow. She asked if I was coming with her?

I wanted to stay here with granddad. Then I wanted to go home with mom and NeNe. First, I said "yes". Mommy got my things ready, then I changed my mind. I don't know what I want to do. I'm confused.

Mommy didn't want to fuss and fight with me so she allowed me to stay. And she said I would have to stay home with grandma tomorrow.

Well, granddad said we are going to go to church tomorrow, Sunday. I don't want to go, but grandma told mommy we are going so, I guess I will have to go. I'm tired, I'm going to sleep. Good night everyone.

Chapter Eleven

I t's another weekend at our grandparents. Grandma brought us some more clothes for school. Mommy and we said thank you.

We had a good evening with our grandparents. Mommy probably had somewhere to go because she left us early after giving us a bath and making sure we ate dinner. It's okay, she deserves a break.

Mommy has been seeming happy lately, I hope I am making her happy not to have any bad notes.

In the morning, grandma woke up, started cleaning up and cooking. We had grits, pancakes, sausage, eggs and cheese.

I didn't eat all my pancakes, so grandma Said, "no grits and cheese, Ty".

Vaeh and I were playing but I started fussing about the games on grandma's phone so she took it away from me. I cried.

After grandma cleaned me and Vaeh up, got us dressed, granddad took Vaeh with him to Valdosta to buy some meat at the meat store. I believe he will stop at my uncle and aunt who live there. But I didn't want to go, so I stayed home with grandma. She didn't want to take the drive either.

But grandma still didn't let me hold the phone because she said I need to learn not to fight my sister and learn how to share. So I turned the tv on and watched the animal channel while grandma worked on her book in the computer room.

I guess I understood, or was I missing my granddad and baby sister?

Later that day, I was outside talking to Goddy. Goddy Benji was cutting my granddads' hedges. Goddy Darlene bought me a toy car. It didn't need a remote. She bought NeNe a doll baby that she could put in the tub and wash.

We both said "thank you Goddy". After we played for a while, I told grandma, "I need to take a bath, I had an accident and wet my pants". I don't like to have anything wet or dirty on me.

She was upset but came with me to be sure I took a good bath. Then NeNe saw me and said she had an accident too.

She had to take a bath. She does mimmick me sometimes.

Grandma said "get ready to go, your mom is coming for you". But I don't want to leave so when mom came, I said, "one more day at school and I am not going back, I want to stay at granddad's house". Everyone looked at me in shock, I don't know why they want me to go to school. I don't like going to school.

But I didn't give mom a hard time this night, I went home, ate dinner and went to bed. I was so tired.

The next day, I lost one of my bottom teeth. I got a good fairy certificate from school for losing my tooth.

I had something good to show to mom, and she told me that I had some homework to do. So we started on that.

Chapter Twelve

On this particular evening, my mom said "Ty let's go, you have to go to school tomorrow", but I was not going to go to school, I just want to stay at my grandparents.

But at least I went home with mommy and Vaeh. And for a few days I was getting good reports. Then a bad report came home. Mommy had to remind my teacher that I had a condition and was being evaluated. That the principal was aware of my condition and that she should have been informed too.

So mommy told her to stop categorizing me and give me a chance to adjust to a new setting.

I did so well in the next few days that mommy gave me my Ipod back. I was Happy, and that keeps me busy at grandma's on the weekend.

This evening my aunt Mary and Ms. Fran came to visit us at grandmas' home.

Grandma invited them over to eat some souse, a good meat stew that southern people love.

They came and ate and ate and enjoyed the dish a lot. When they left, we played with my granddad. Grandma was busy writing in her book.

Vaeh cried when they left because grandma gave them some crackers that she liked and they did not give them back to her. She did not know, it was because she never really ate them.

Later, Vaeh sat with grandma and ate grapes. She loves grapes. Vaeh admitted to grandma that she and I had dialed the phone in the computer room. She talks a lot.

So grandma told me to stay off the phone in the computer room. Of course, I said, "I didn't play on that phone". Anyway, my grandma knows.

Mommy came to get us. It's time to go home. She just got her car back after 6 weeks in the shop. Thank God they did what needed to be done so we could be safe going to school and work.

I'm doing better, I was ready to go with mommy. Though I took forever putting my shoes on and then I wanted something to eat. Mommy is always patient, waiting for me by the door with so much in her arms. I love my mommy.

Vaeh is coaxing me, "come on boy, put your shoes on, mommy is ready to go".

"Okay", I said, then we were on our way home.

Ty got in trouble today. The teacher called his mom and said that he was bullying a student all day, later turned to the student and pushed him down.

Something is wrong with this picture. I understand, Ty is not perfect and may get off task but to be told that he bullied a child all day and the teacher did nothing to him, and that he pushed a child down. Uhh, I don't think so. The principal and mommy need to talk. Let's get to the bottom of this.

Monday, mommy and granddad will meet with the Principal of my elementary school. This teacher has something against me. Even my classmate told mommy that she saw the whole thing.

When asked to explain what she saw, she said she saw our classmate beating me in the back and told mommy that the teacher sent the boy to the Principal's office.

Mommy is not happy, but grandma says, "this teacher is going to be in trouble". And I believe her. How could she so call, let me bully this boy all day, never separate us, then when he hits me, she only sends the boy to the office? "Really?". Did I do what the teacher said I did earlier?

Chapter Thirteen

Today, mommy was supposed to work a double. She thought about us, got off work early and took us to a big park. We got on the big slide and had lots of fun. When we came back, mommy gave me and Vaeh a bath and asked what did we want to eat.

Vaeh said mac and cheese, I said "pancakes". When mommy gave me the pancakes, I cried and said, "I wanted mac and cheese". She hesitantly gave it to me, but I cried and said "I don't want that I said, pancakes".

Mommy was so mad at me, she left the food on the towel, but I would not eat it, so I went to sleep without eating.

When morning came, I was so hungry and had a headache. I told grandma, I wanted medicine for my head because it was hurting.

Grandma felt I just needed to eat and she fixed us some food. I asked for mac and cheese, Vaeh wanted pancakes.

When grandma gave me the mac and cheese, I said, "I don't want that, I said I wanted pancakes".

Grandma ignored me, and I ate my mac and cheese. She always takes us outside so we can tire ourselves out, come in, wash up, and take a nap.

Today, I was trying to pull my bike out, granddad said don't try to ride it because it has a flat. But when I tried to pull it out with one hand and something in the other hand, I fell on the end of the handle bar and injured my stomach.

Grandma checked me out, bandaged me up and kept an eye on my wound. After awhile, it was not looking too good, so she called mommy to come and get me to get checked out.

She brought us in the house, gave us a bath and got us ready for mommy to pick us up.

Mommy had to leave work early, and I fought not to go with her, but granddaddy soon convinced me to get in the car and go to the doctors.

The doctor said, it's a good thing that my stomach is soft and not hard. Just check me for blood in the urine and showing pain. Give me some pain medicine if necessary, because it is just a bruise. Mommy and grandma are relieved.

We played hard today, inspite of my injury. So after the doctors, we went straight to sleep and will sleep until time to get up for school tomorrow. Good nite.

When Tuesday rolled around, mommy told me in the morning that I had a dentist appointment.

I had a great day in school. Mommy had an appointment with the principal and my team, who would be evaluating me.

She came to get me from my kindergarten class. When I saw mommy, I started crying. As she called for me, I said "no", "I'm not going with you, I'm going to my other school", the Nursery.

The Principal, school psychologist, team teachers and mommy tried to calm me. I slapped the teacher who got in my face.

When mom tried to chastise me, I kicked her twice. She was so upset and crying but I was not going with mommy. I forgot she said I had an appointment, and no body reminded me that she was coming for me.

After a while, I sat on the ground and cried, and cried, they took turns trying to calm me down. I was sweating and hitting at anyone who came near me.

Finally, granddaddy came, my mom had called him, and I eventually calmed down.

They were talking about my behavior. That mom is doing what she can and I could not help what was going on. After the doctor's visit, I am labeled Attention Deficit Hyperactivity Disorder (ADHD) and Oppositional Defiance Disorder (ODD).

But at least they are going to put me in a class with less kids to try to work on my problem. God help me and help mommy.

Mommy is a little relieved that they told her she was doing everything right.

And that they would change the time that I take my medication so it would work at both schools, because I was taking it at 6:30 before going to the nursery. Now I will take it at 8:30 when I get to the Elementary.

Later in the evening, mom called my grandparents. I heard mommy say, "they are working with him, the whole team of psychologist, principal and teachers.

Mommy didn't know I heard her, but I ran over to her, gave her a big hug around the waist and said "I love you mommy".

I heard her tell my grandparents that I shocked her. I am still confused at some of the things that I do, but I love my mom.

Grandma thought she might end this part of my story, until she saw the tape that mommy filmed at my school.

Again, she saw another side of me. I am not my loving self, but I don't know why not. Grandma continues to pray for me. I'm sure that one day, we will all understand it by and by. Knowing my grandma, she won't stop until she finds out, what triggers my behavior.

I love you grandma and I know you love me, Ty.

Summative

"Ty", Through Grandma's Eyes

I am a little boy, lost yet found to be just, in (GOD), my father's sight. Just, in my grandma's eyes and approved by the almighty.

I once was lost, but now I am found. I am claiming it in the name of Jesus Christ our Saviour.

I want to believe that I was just misunderstood by some, mistaken by none and not accused by any.

I try to be loving as my mommy taught me to love, to respect as my granddad taught me to respect, to share as my baby sister told me I should.

My grandma prayed and she always said that God hears the prayers of the righteous. My grandma prayed for me and in due season she said, I will reap what I sowed, she taught me this. I don't want to take medicine for the rest of my life, so God, fix me sooner than later. Amen.

My Prayer:

Dear God, raise me up to be the young man of valour that you purposed for me, and allow me to be happy, humble and healthy as grandma prayed. God, please protect me, mommy, Vaeh and my entire loving family. And oh God, lay your hands on my dad, whom I love also. Amen.

Though the episodes continue, even as my granddad was called to get me to calm down tonight. I was very upset that I couldn't go outside to play ball because I left my homework folder at school. When mom tried to get me to go inside, I hit my sister in the face, kicked mommy a couple of times and screamed at the top of my lungs until my granddad came.

But God, I still know you will work a miracle in me. Amen.

Author's Notes

This is not just another story being told. It is a story of trust, courage, bravery, purity, and confidence exhibited by Ty, Tracy and grandma.

We all trust God to turn this situation around. We, including granddad had courage to deal with the situation at hand as it relates to Ty. Ty is brave and tries to do the right things when his mind is not baffled. He is a pure, innocent child caught up in this illness.

We are confident that someday, I will be writing another story of how Ty made it over and how proud we are of him to have continued to strive for greatness.

Tracy and I know that someday, her son will do great things that will help the next child with ADHD and ODD, with the help of the Lord.

How To Cope With A Bipolar Child:

N ever yell, get angry or punish. This will only make the situation worse or spark an episode.

Try to understand what in particular upset the child and get the child to talk about it.

Allow him to speak freely and just listen.

Everydayhealthadvisor.com

They generally exude extreme anger that can last for hours, risk-seeking and dangerous behavior, and an extreme reaction to any kind of parental boundaries.

References

EverydayHealthAdvisor.com
Proverbs 22:6 KJV
Romans 8:28 NASB
Proverbs 3:5-6 NIV
John 14:14 KJV